Walking in His Love

30-DAY DEVOTIONAL FOR GOD'S DAUGHTERS

LAPASHA WHITE

Credits

Walking in His Love: A 30-Day Devotional for God's Daughters

Author: Lapasha White

Publisher: Independently published

Disclaimer: The views and opinions expressed in this book are those of the author and do not necessarily reflect the official policy or position of any individual or organization mentioned within.

ISBN: 9798869138019
Printed in the United States of America

DEDICATION

This book is dedicated to my Heavenly Father, a Father like no other. I am forever grateful for how You pulled me out of some of the darkest places and gave me such peace. Your love has never left me nor forsaking me. I also dedicate this book to my family. I love and cherish you all.

I REALLY
NEED A DAY
BETWEEN
SATURDAY
& SUNDAY

CONTENTS

Introduction

hey yall!

I'm Lapasha! Thank you from the depths of my heart for choosing to embark on the transformative journey with "Walking in His Love: A 30-Day Devotional for God's Daughters." Your decision to dive into these pages is not only an investment in yourself but also a declaration of your desire to walk hand in hand with your Heavenly Father, basking in His unwavering love and discovering the remarkable depths of your identity as His cherished daughter.

As you journey through these devotionals, may you experience the profound embrace of His love, find comfort in His refuge, radiate His compassion, and anchor yourself in the timeless truths of His Word. I believe that as you allow these words to guide you, you'll uncover the beauty of your purpose and the strength that comes from knowing you are deeply loved.

Thank you for your trust and dedication to becoming the woman you were created to be. I eagerly wait to see your transformation as you continue to blossom as a radiant daughter of the King.

With love, Lapasha

Week 1:

EMBRACING *your* IDENTITY *in* LOVE

Explore the depths of your identity as a cherished daughter of God and discover the profound significance of His love in shaping who you are.

Embracing Your Identity

"I praise You because I am fearfully and wonderfully made; Your works are wonderful, I know that full well."
Psalm 139:14

DEAR DAUGHTER OF GOD,

Today marks the beginning of a transformative journey where we dive deep into the incredible relationship you share with your Heavenly Father. To start, let's embrace the truth that you are not an accident or an afterthought; you are an intentional creation of God.

With every fiber of your being, you have been carefully and thoughtfully crafted by the hands of the Creator. Just as an earthly father cherishes his child, your Heavenly Father takes delight in you. Your unique qualities, talents, and experiences are a masterpiece in His eyes.

Take a moment today to reflect on the details that make you who you are, and offer heartfelt gratitude to God for shaping you in His image.

PRAYER:

Dear Heavenly Father,
As I begin this journey, I thank You for the love with which You've uniquely crafted me. Open my heart to fully embrace the identity You've given me as Your beloved daughter. May Your love shape my understanding of self, grounding me in the assurance of Your unwavering affection. In Jesus name, I pray. Amen.

What Does This Reveal About God?

Psalm 139:14 uncovers the profound truth about God's role as the intentional Creator. It speaks of the details and purpose that is put into every individual's existence. **God, the Heavenly Father, is revealed as an artist thoroughly crafting each person with care and love. Psalm 139:14 reveals a God who takes joy in the uniqueness of His creation, finding beauty in every detail.** It showcases the divine intentionality behind every life, reflecting a love that goes beyond comprehension.

How Can I Apply This to My Life?

As a daughter of God, recognizing that you are fearfully and wonderfully made involves a shift in perspective. **Take time to reflect on the details of your identity – your qualities, talents, and experiences – and see them as intentional aspects of God's creative design.** Embrace gratitude for the way God has shaped you.

In your daily life, carry the awareness that you are a masterpiece in God's eyes. Let this understanding influence your self-perception, actions, and interactions with others. By fully embracing your identity, you align yourself with the truth of God's unwavering love, finding strength and purpose in being His beloved daughter.

"Embrace your identity as a daughter of God. Your uniqueness is a masterpiece woven by the Creator of the universe."

Who or what has influenced your understanding of your identity, and how might embracing your identity as a daughter of God reshape your self-perception?

Seeking God's Presence

"Come near to God and He will come near to you."
James 4:8

BELOVED DAUGHTER,

Drawing closer to your Heavenly Father is a journey that begins with a heart that seeks earnestly. Imagine a father longing for his child's presence; that's how God longs for you.

As you approach Him, remember that He is already moving towards you. **The Creator of the universe desires intimacy with you.**

Today, spend some time in prayer and meditation, intentionally seeking His presence. **Open your heart to hear His voice, knowing that your pursuit of Him does not go unnoticed.** Your Heavenly Father desires to reveal more of Himself to you.

PRAYER:

Heavenly Father,
In the quiet moments of this day, draw me into Your loving presence. Help me seek You above all else, recognizing that in Your presence, there is fullness of joy. May my day be centered on communing with You, my source of peace and guidance. In Jesus name, I pray. Amen.

What Does This Reveal About God?

The imagery of a father longing for his child's presence reveals the deep, personal, and emotional connection God desires with each of His children. **It describes a God who actively seeks intimacy, expressing a heartfelt longing for communion with each of His daughters.** This revelation highlights the relational nature of God, emphasizing His desire for a close and personal relationship with those who earnestly seek Him.

How Can I Apply This to My Life?

Embracing the idea of God longing for your presence invites you into a deeper, more intentional relationship with Him. Recognize that, just as a child's presence brings joy to a parent, your presence brings joy to your Heavenly Father.

Today, **intentionally set aside time for prayer and meditation.** Seek God's presence with an open heart, knowing that He is already moving towards you. In this sacred space, listen for His voice, feel His love, and allow His peace to fill your heart. **Make seeking God's presence a daily practice**, and watch as your relationship with Him reach new depths, becoming an undeniable source of joy, peace, and guidance in your life.

"In the stillness, God's presence is found. Seek Him earnestly, for in His company, you will find rest and renewal."

Reflect on a time when you felt particularly close to God. What elements contributed to that sense of nearness, and how can you intentionally seek His presence daily?

The Father's Love

"See what great love the Father has lavished on us, that we should be called children of God!"
1 John 3:1

PRECIOUS DAUGHTER,

As you embark on this journey, it's vital to anchor yourself in the understanding of God's immense love for you. Imagine a father gazing at his child with an overflowing heart of affection; that's how your Heavenly Father looks at you.

God's love knows no bounds, and He has chosen to adopt you as His own. Every moment, He lavishes His love upon you, and you are entrusted with the privilege of being called a child of God.

Reflect on this truth today and let God's love shape your identity and your understanding of your worth.

PRAYER:

Loving Father,
Thank You for the boundless love You shower upon me. As I reflect on Your love today, let it spill over into every aspect of my being. Help me comprehend the depth of Your affection and respond to others with the same love You've graciously given me. In Jesus' name, I pray. Amen.

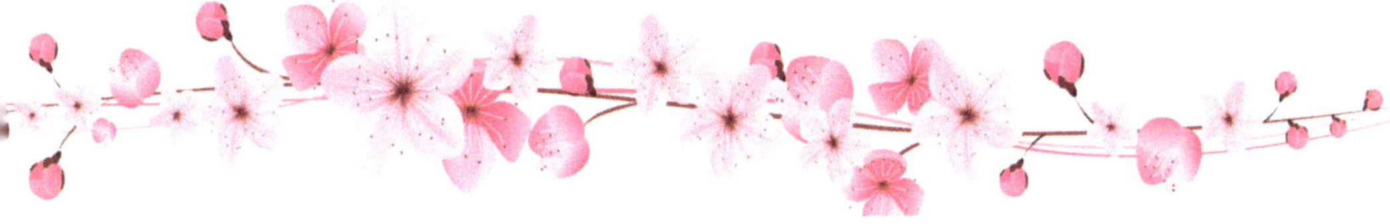

What Does This Reveal About God?

The symbolism of a father gazing at his child with overflowing affection reveals the profound, boundless love of God. It communicates the concept that **God's love is not solely based on sentiment but a deep, enduring, and unconditional love.**

This revelation reveals a Father who delights in His children, choosing them as His own and showering them with love. It highlights the foundational truth that **you are a beloved daughter of God, cherished beyond measure, not because you have earned it but because your Heavenly Father has chosen to love you** unconditionally long before you did anything to earn it.

How Can I Apply This to My Life?

Anchoring yourself in the understanding of God's immense love is transformative. **Take time today to reflect on the truth that you are adopted into God's family, chosen and dearly loved. Allow this realization to shape your identity and self-worth.**

As you go about your day, let the awareness of God's boundless love influence your interactions with others. Respond to others with the same love you've received from your Heavenly Father, extending grace and compassion. Embrace the privilege of being called a child of God, living in the assurance of His unconditional and overflowing love.

"God's love is a relentless current that carries you through every season. You are His cherished daughter, held in His loving embrace."

Let's Reflect

How does the idea of being a beloved daughter of God impact
the way you view His love for you? In what ways can you allow
His love to influence your thoughts and actions today?

Trusting Your Father

"Trust in the Lord with all your heart and lean not on your own understanding; in all your ways submit to Him, and He will make your paths straight."
Proverbs 3:5-6

SUBMITTED DAUGHTER,

Trusting God is a cornerstone of your relationship with Him. Imagine a father guiding his child along unfamiliar paths, holding her hand in unwavering assurance; that's how your Heavenly Father guides you.

He invites you to trust His wisdom and plans, even when they don't align with your own. Just as a child relies on her father's guidance, place your trust in God's capable hands.

As you submit to God's leading, He will pave a path that aligns with His perfect will for your life.

PRAYER:

Dear Lord,
I entrust my day into Your loving hands. Teach me to trust Your guidance and provision, knowing that as my Heavenly Father, You are faithful. In moments of uncertainty, I choose to rely on Your wisdom and love, confident that Your plans for me are filled with hope. In Jesus name, I pray. Amen.

What Does This Reveal About God?

The imagery of a father guiding his child along unfamiliar paths, holding her hand in unwavering assurance, reveals the trustworthy and guiding nature of God. **It reveals a Heavenly Father who invites His daughters to trust His wisdom and plans, even in the face of uncertainty.** This speaks to God's faithfulness and His desire for a relationship built on trust, where you can confidently rely on His guidance and provision.

How Can I Apply This to My Life?

Trusting God as your Heavenly Father is a foundational aspect of your relationship with Him. Today, embrace the image of God guiding you along life's paths. **In moments of uncertainty, consciously choose to submit to His lead, trusting that His plans for you are filled with hope.**

As you go about your day, release any anxieties or doubts into His capable hands. **Practice relying on His wisdom and love, knowing that, like a loving father, He is faithful to guide you in the paths that align with His perfect will for your life.**

"Trust in the Lord's plan, for He leads you with a perfect love that casts out all fear."

Consider an area of your life where trust may be challenging.
How can recognizing God as your trustworthy Father reshape
your perspective and approach to trust?

Renewing Your Mind

"Do not conform to the pattern of this world, but be transformed by the renewing of your mind."
Romans 12:2

RENEWED DAUGHTER,

In a world filled with noise and distractions, cultivating a strong connection with your Heavenly Father requires the intentional renewal of your mind.

Imagine a father teaching his child to discern right from wrong, guiding her to make wise choices; that's how God desires to transform your thinking.

His Word is a beacon of truth in the midst of confusion. Just as a child absorbs her father's teachings, immerse yourself in Scripture to renew your mind.

Allow His truth to shape your thoughts, choices, and perspective, enabling you to see the world through His eyes.

PRAYER:

Heavenly Father,
Today, I invite Your Holy Spirit to transform my mind. Help me break free from negative thought patterns and align my thinking with Your truth. Let Your Word dwell richly in my heart, shaping my perspectives and renewing my mind to be more like Yours. In Jesus name, I pray. Amen.

What Does This Reveal About God?

The example of a father teaching his child to discern right from wrong, guiding her to make wise choices, reveals God's desire to actively transform and renew your mind. **It communicates the Father's role in helping His daughters navigate the complexities of life by providing a source of truth in the midst of confusion.** God's Word is depicted as a reliable guide, shaping your thinking and enabling you to make choices that align with the wisdom and nature of God.

How Can I Apply This to My Life?

In a world filled with distractions and conflicting messages, intentionally renewing your mind is crucial. Picture God guiding you to discern right from wrong, just as a loving father would. Today, **immerse yourself in Scripture to allow His truth to extend beyond your thoughts, feelings, and perspective.**

As you go about your day, **be conscious of negative thought patterns and actively replace them with God's truth.** Let His Word dwell richly in your heart, shaping your perspective to align more closely with His.

"Transform your mind with the truth of God's Word. As you think, so shall you become."

What thought patterns or beliefs might be hindering your spiritual growth? How can you actively renew your mind with God's truth?

Finding Rest

"Come to me, all you who are weary and burdened, and I will give you rest."
Matthew 11:28-30

RESTED DAUGHTER,

Imagine a father offering his child solace in his arms after a tiring day, soothing her worries with his gentle words; that's how your Heavenly Father offers you rest.

In the midst of life's demands, you can find rest in God's presence. Like a caring father, He beckons you to come to Him with your weariness and burdens.

Release your cares to Him and allow His peace to envelop your heart. As you rest in Him, you'll find restoration for your soul.

PRAYER:

Lord of Peace,
As I seek rest in Your presence, quiet the noise around me. Grant me a sense of deep rest in Your love. In the midst of busyness, help me find moments of quiet reflection and rejuvenation. May Your peace permeate my soul today. In Jesus' name, I pray. Amen.

What Does This Reveal About God?

The imagery of a father offering comfort to his tired child reveals the nurturing and comforting nature of God. **It paints a picture of a Heavenly Father who cares deeply about the weariness His daughters may feel.** His invitation to find rest in His presence reflects His desire for an intimate, soothing relationship with each of His children. In this, God showcases His role as a source of peace and restoration.

How Can I Apply This to My Life?

In the midst of life's demands, actively seek moments of rest in God's presence. Picture yourself coming to your Heavenly Father with your weariness and burdens, much like a child approaching a caring father.

As you go about your day, make a conscious effort to release your cares to God. Whenever you feel overwhelmed, pause and breathe in His peace as you exhale your burdens. Place them in the hands of your Father and trust that He is working it all out because He cares for you. **Embrace moments of quiet reflection and rejuvenation, allowing God's love to envelop your heart, bringing a sense of deep rest.**

"Rest is a gift from God, a pause in which you can bask in His love and emerge recharged."

Let's Reflect

In what areas of your life do you need rest? How can you intentionally create space for rest and rejuvenation in God's love?

Walking in Obedience

"But if anyone obeys His word, love for God is truly made complete in them. This is how we know we are in Him: Whoever claims to live in Him must live as Jesus did."
John 2:5-6

OBEDIENT DAUGHTER,

Obedience to God's Word is an act of love and devotion. **Imagine a father guiding his child, teaching her values and principles that shape her character; that's how your Heavenly Father guides you through His Word.**

Imitating Jesus, the perfect example of a life lived in obedience, is your goal. Just as a child trusts her father's wisdom, trust in the wisdom of God's Word.

As you seek to align your life with His teachings, your love for Him will be made complete, and your bond with your Heavenly Father will flourish.

PRAYER:

Father,
Guide my steps in paths of righteousness. Give me the strength to walk in obedience to Your Word and Your will. May my actions and choices reflect the love and obedience of a devoted daughter. In Jesus name, I pray. Amen.

What Does This Reveal About God?

The analogy of a father guiding his child and teaching values and principles illustrates **God as a loving guide and instructor. God, in His Word, provides a roadmap for life, offering guidance on how to navigate challenges and make choices aligned with His word.** His desire is not to restrict you. He's not trying to suffocate you with rules but instead He is a Father who desires to protect and lead His daughter into a life of purpose, joy, and fulfillment through obedience.

How Can I Apply This to My Life?

Imagine yourself as a child learning valuable life lessons from a wise and caring father. Approach God's Word with the intention of understanding His character, His principles and His values. Trust in the wisdom embedded in His Word, just as a child trusts their father's guidance. Seek opportunities in your daily life to align your actions with the principles outlined in the Bible. **Remember that God is not giving you a standard to live by because He wants to hinder you or "box you in". Your obedience to God's word and/or instructions are for your protection.**

Ultimately God wants to perfect you to be made in the image of Christ. Your Heavenly Father wants you to access and live the abundant life He has created for you. This requires your ability to obey and trust in Him. As you strive to live in obedience, your love for God will deepen, and your relationship with Him will flourish.

"Obedience to God's Word is a step toward becoming the woman He designed you to be."

Reflect on a time when obedience led to positive outcomes in your life. How does walking in obedience to God align with your identity as His daughter?

End of Week 1
ENCOURAGEMENT:

As we wrap up the first week of 'Walking in His Love: A 30-Day Devotional for God's Daughters,' take a moment to reflect on the incredible journey you've embarked upon.

Just as a flower opens to the warmth of the sun, you've been opening your heart to the love of your Heavenly Father.

Let the seeds of truth you've planted this week continue to grow, and may your spirit be refreshed as you head into the coming week.

Remember, you are His cherished daughter, and His love is your foundation. Stay strong, keep the faith, and know that your journey is just beginning.

What aspects of your identity have you struggled to fully embrace? How does knowing you're a beloved daughter of God impact these struggles?

How does recognizing yourself as a daughter of God influence
your perspective on your purpose and worth?

What practical steps can you take to daily remind yourself of
your identity in Christ?

Week 2:

FINDING
STRENGTH
in LOVE'S
Refuge

Dive into the rest and strength that God's love offers, finding refuge and renewal in His presence as you navigate life's challenges.

A Heart of Gratitude

"Give thanks in all circumstances; for this is God's will for you in Christ Jesus."
1 Thessalonians 5:18

GRATEFUL DAUGHTER,

Imagine a child thanking her father for every gift, every meal, and every moment of his love; that's the attitude of gratitude your Heavenly Father desires from you. As you journey with Him, cultivate a heart that overflows with thankfulness.

Gratitude isn't just about giving thanks for the good times, but also about acknowledging God's presence and provision even in challenging circumstances.

Just as a father's heart swells when his child expresses gratitude, your Heavenly Father delights in your thankful heart. Practice gratitude daily and discover the joy it brings to your relationship with God.

PRAYER:

Gracious God,
Thank You for the countless blessings that surround me. Today, cultivate within me a heart of gratitude. Open my eyes to see Your goodness in every circumstance, and may my heart overflow with thanksgiving for Your love and provision. In Jesus' name, I pray. Amen.

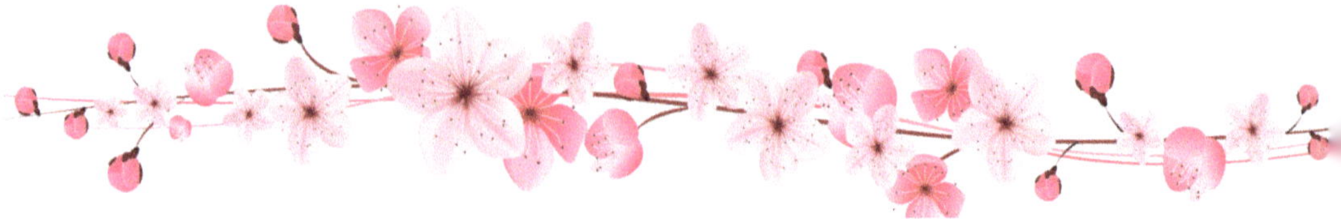

What Does This Reveal About God?

The comparison of a child expressing gratitude to her father reflects **God's desire for His daughters to approach Him with thankful hearts.** God is not just interested in receiving praise during moments of joy. He also desires an ongoing attitude of gratitude. Your Heavenly Father appreciates when you acknowledge and show admiration for His presence, provision, and love, nurturing a deeper connection between Him and His beloved daughters.

How Can I Apply This to My Life?

Visualize yourself as a child expressing gratitude to a loving father for every aspect of life. Cultivate a daily practice of thankfulness, acknowledging both the blessings and the challenges. Make it a habit to thank God not only for the obvious joys but also for His sustaining grace in difficult times. **As you embrace a heart of gratitude, you'll find that your relationship with your Heavenly Father will reach greater depths, and joy becomes a constant companion.**

"Gratitude unlocks the door to joy. Each thanksgiving deepens your connection to Your Heavenly Father."

Let's Reflect

Take stock of the blessings in your life. How might cultivating a heart of gratitude deepen your connection with God and others?

Forgiving as He Forgave

"Be kind and compassionate to one another, forgiving each other,
just as in Christ God forgave you."
Ephesians 4:32

FORGIVEN DAUGHTER,

Imagine a father extending forgiveness to his child after a mistake, wiping away tears and fostering reconciliation; that's the mercy your Heavenly Father extends to you.

Forgiveness is a powerful aspect of your relationship with God and others. Just as a child learns from her father's example of forgiveness, embrace the call to forgive as Christ forgave you.

Release the burden of resentment and hurt, letting love and compassion mend relationships. In forgiving, you reflect the heart of your Heavenly Father.

PRAYER:

Merciful Father,
As I reflect on Your forgiveness, empower me to extend the same grace to others. Release any bitterness from my heart, and help me forgive as You have forgiven me. May Your love guide my responses and actions. In Jesus name, I pray. Amen.

What Does This Reveal About God?

The image of a father extending forgiveness to his child illustrates God's boundless mercy and His role as the ultimate Source of forgiveness. **Our Heavenly Father is quick to forgive, wiping away our mistakes and fostering reconciliation.**

Psalm 86:15 reminds us, "But you, O Lord, are a God merciful and gracious, slow to anger and abounding in steadfast love and faithfulness. **God's forgiveness is a profound expression of His love and a testament to His desire for restored relationships with His daughters.**

How Can I Apply This to My Life?

Imagine yourself as a child receiving forgiveness from a loving father, and in turn, extending that forgiveness to others. Embrace the transformative power of forgiveness in your relationships. **Release the burden of resentment and hurt, choosing love and compassion instead.** As you practice forgiveness, you mirror the heart of your Heavenly Father, cultivating healing and restoration in your connections with others.

*"Forgiveness breaks chains and restores hearts.
As a daughter of grace, extend forgiveness as your
Heavenly Father has done for you."*

Is there someone you need to forgive? How does God's forgiveness of you inspire and guide your forgiveness of others?

Growing in Faith

"Now faith is confidence in what we hope for and assurance about what we do not see."
Hebrews 11:1

FAITHFUL DAUGHTER,

Imagine a child taking her father's hand to cross a bridge even when she can't see what lies ahead; that's the essence of faith that God desires from you.

Faith is the foundation of your relationship with your Heavenly Father. Just as a child trusts her father's guidance, **trust in the promises of God even when circumstances seem uncertain.** Let your faith grow stronger as you rely on His unfailing love and guidance.

In times of doubt, remember the countless examples of faithfulness throughout Scripture (I provide a few examples on the next page) **and allow them to inspire your journey of faith.**

PRAYER:

Faithful God,
Today, I choose to grow in faith. Strengthen my trust in You, even in the face of uncertainties. Let my faith be an anchor in the storms of life, grounded in the certainty of Your love and promises. In Jesus name, I pray. Amen.

What Does This Reveal About God?

The imagery of a child taking her father's hand to cross a bridge illustrates God's desire for our unwavering faith in Him. **Like a trustworthy father guiding his child, God calls His daughters to trust in His promises, even when the path ahead is unclear.** God's faithfulness becomes the **anchor** of our own faith, providing a solid foundation for our relationship with Him.

How Can I Apply This to My Life?

Visualize yourself taking God's hand and stepping forward in faith, even when you can't see the full picture. Trust in His promises and allow your faith to grow stronger as you rely on His unfailing love and guidance.

In moments of doubt, turn to the examples of faithfulness found in Scripture for inspiration. Here's a few to get you started:

"Daniels 6:4 states that Daniel remained steadfast in his faith, enduring the scrutiny of his enemies who sought to find fault in him, yet they discovered no wrongdoing. Similarly, Abraham and Sarah patiently waited for 25 years for God to fulfill His promise of granting them a son, a narrative found in Genesis chapters 17 to 21."

By cultivating a growing faith, you deepen your connection with your Heavenly Father.

"Faith is your anchor in the storm, your assurance in the unseen. Let it bloom and guide you."

Consider a recent challenge. In what ways can faith be your anchor in navigating difficulties?

Day 11

Abiding in His Word

"If you remain in Me and My words remain in you, ask whatever you wish, and it will be done for you."
John 15:7

WORD-FILLED DAUGHTER,

Imagine a father imparting his wisdom to his child through stories and teachings, guiding her decisions and actions; that's the significance of God's Word in your life. Just as a child treasures her father's teachings, treasure the words of Scripture in your heart.

Abiding in God's Word means allowing it to shape your thoughts, desires, and actions. As you immerse yourself in His truth, your prayers align with His will, and your connection with your Heavenly Father deepens.

The promises and insights found in His Word become a constant source of guidance and comfort on your journey.

PRAYER:

Heavenly Father,
As I dive into Your Word, may it become a lamp to my feet and a light to my path. Let Your truth dwell richly in my heart, guiding my thoughts and actions. May I abide in Your Word, finding strength and wisdom in its pages. In Jesus name, I pray. Amen.

What Does This Reveal About God?

God's Word is not merely a collection of stories; it is a profound source of wisdom and guidance, much like a loving father imparting invaluable lessons to his child. Just as a father's teachings shape a child's decisions and actions, God's Word is meant to profoundly influence our lives. **The Scriptures reflect His unwavering love, timeless truths, and a desire for a deep, personal connection with each of His children.**

How Can I Apply This to My Life?

To abide in God's Word is to treasure and internalize it, allowing its principles to shape your thoughts, desires, and actions. Regularly spend time reading, meditating, and reflecting on Scripture. As you do, seek to understand the profound truths it contains and let them guide your daily decisions.

Align your prayers with the promises and wisdom found in God's Word. By making Scripture a constant companion on your journey, you deepen your connection with your Heavenly Father and gain a timeless source of guidance and comfort.

"God's Word is a lamp to your path, guiding your steps with wisdom and truth."

How consistently do you engage with God's Word? How might a deeper connection with His Word impact your daily life?

A Heart of Compassion

"Therefore, as God's chosen people, holy and dearly loved, clothe yourselves with compassion, kindness, humility, gentleness, and patience."
Colossians 3:12

COMPASSIONATE DAUGHTER,

Imagine a child reflecting her father's heart of compassion by helping those in need, offering kindness and empathy; that's how your Heavenly Father encourages you to live.

Just as a child emulates her father's compassion, clothe yourself with compassion, kindness, humility, gentleness, and patience. These virtues reflect the nature of God and His love for His children.

Allow His compassion to flow through you, touching the lives of those around you. **Your actions and words become a testament to the compassionate heart of your Heavenly Father.**

PRAYER:

Compassionate God,
Open my heart to the needs of others. Help me embody Your compassion, extending kindness and understanding to those around me. May Your love flow through me, touching lives with the warmth of Your compassion. In Jesus name, I pray. Amen.

What Does This Reveal About God?

The heart of God is characterized by boundless compassion. In the same way, a child learns from her father's compassion and then reflects that compassion by helping those in need, God invites His children to embody compassion in their lives. **This aspect of God's nature emphasizes His love for humanity and His desire for His children to express that love through acts of kindness, empathy, humility, gentleness, and patience.**

How Can I Apply This to My Life?

To live with a heart of compassion is to echo God's compassionate nature. Clothe yourself with compassion, kindness, humility, gentleness, and patience, allowing these virtues to guide your interactions. Actively seek opportunities to help those in need, demonstrating empathy and kindness. In doing so, you become a living testament to the compassionate heart of your Heavenly Father. **Let your actions and words be a reflection of His boundless love and compassion.**

"Compassion is a reflection of His heart. Let your actions speak His love to a hurting world."

Let's Reflect

Think of a situation where you've shown compassion. How does expressing compassion align with your identity as God's daughter?

<h1 style="text-align:center">Day 13</h1>

Bearing Fruit

"You did not choose me, but I chose you and appointed you so that you might go and bear fruit—fruit that will last."
John 15:16

FRUITFUL DAUGHTER,

Imagine a father tending to a garden with his child, nurturing each plant to produce abundant and lasting fruit; that's how your Heavenly Father tends to your growth.

He chose you and has appointed you to bear fruit that brings glory to His name. Just as a child participates in her father's gardening, cooperate with God's work in your life.

Seek His guidance to discover the unique ways you can bear fruit that has an eternal impact. **As you align your life with His purpose, you'll find fulfillment and joy in producing lasting, fruit that glorifies your Father's name.**

PRAYER:

Heavenly Father,
As I abide in You, may my life bear fruit that glorifies Your name. Cultivate within me the qualities of love, joy, peace, patience, kindness, goodness, faithfulness, gentleness, and self-control. May my life be a testimony to Your transformative power. In Jesus name, I pray. Amen.

What Does This Reveal About God?

God, as the divine gardener, is invested in nurturing the growth of His children. Like a father tending to the overall growth and development of his child, God is actively involved in fostering spiritual development.

The metaphor of bearing fruit illustrates God's desire for His children to yield abundant and lasting results that bring glory to His name. **This reveals a God who is intentional in His plans for each individual, desiring a fruitful and purposeful life for His children.**

How Can I Apply This to My Life?

Recognize that you are chosen and appointed by God to bear fruit in your life. Embrace your role in cooperating with God's work, seeking His guidance to understand the unique ways you can bear fruit with eternal significance. **Align your life with His purpose through prayer, studying His Word, and seeking His will.** As you actively participate in God's plan, you'll find fulfillment and joy in producing lasting, fruit that glorifies His name.

"Your life is a garden of God's love. Nurture it, and watch the fruits of His Spirit flourish."

In what areas of your life would you like to see more spiritual fruit? How can you nurture growth in those areas?

Finding Joy

"You make known to me the path of life; you will fill me with joy in your presence, with eternal pleasures at your right hand."
Psalm 16:11

JOYFUL DAUGHTER,

Imagine a child dancing in her father's embrace, finding joy in his company and unwavering love; that's the joy your Heavenly Father offers you.

In His presence, there is fullness of joy. Just as a child finds delight in her father's love, find joy in spending time with your Heavenly Father. Seek His presence through prayer, worship, and meditation.

As you draw near to Him, His joy becomes your strength, uplifting you in times of sorrow and infusing every aspect of your life with radiant joy.

PRAYER:

God of Joy,
In Your presence is fullness of joy. Today, I choose joy in every circumstance, knowing that Your joy is my strength. Help me find delight in Your love and the blessings You have given me. In Jesus name, I pray. Amen.

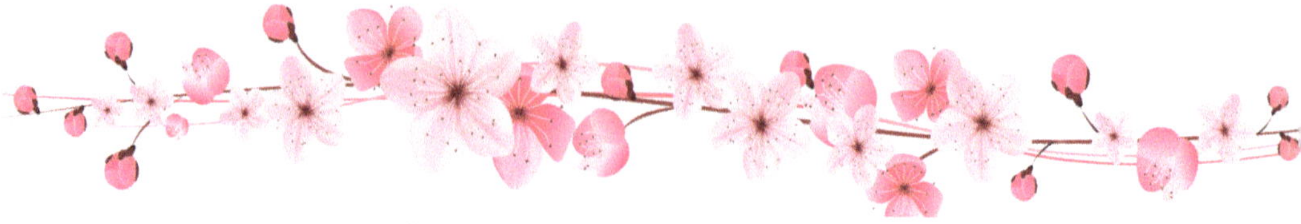

What Does This Reveal About God?

God, as the ultimate Source of joy, invites His children into a relationship where joy is abundant and transformative. The image of a child dancing in her father's embrace reflects the joy found in the presence of the Heavenly Father. **God's joy is not depended on circumstances but is a constant and overflowing aspect of His nature. This reveals a God who desires His children to experience a profound and sustaining joy that originates from being close to Him.** Scripture says that in God's presence there is fullness of joy (Psalm 16:11).

How Can I Apply This to My Life?

Cultivate a habit of seeking joy in God's presence. Set aside time for prayer, worship, and meditation, where you can draw near to your Heavenly Father. **Recognize that His joy becomes your strength, lifting you up in challenging times.** Develop an awareness of the joy that comes from your relationship with your Heavenly Father, allowing it to overflow into every aspect of your life. In moments of sorrow or difficulty, intentionally turn to God's presence to experience the sustaining joy He offers.

"Joy is a melody that sings through adversity. Find it in His presence and share it with the world."

Reflect on the sources of joy in your life. How can you share that joy with others today?

End of Week 2
ENCOURAGEMENT:

Congratulations on completing two weeks of 'Walking in His Love: A 30-Day Devotional for God's Daughters'! As you've delved deeper into the understanding of God's love, you're becoming more rooted in your identity as His beloved daughter.

Just as a tree strengthens its roots to withstand storms, you're grounding yourself in the unshakable love of your Heavenly Father. As you rest this weekend, let the truth of His love continue to rejuvenate your spirit.

May the seeds of His Word bear fruit in your life, bringing you joy, strength, and a deeper connection with Him.

Reflection Questions

When have you felt the most restful and rejuvenated in God's presence? How can you prioritize and cultivate more of these moments?

How does knowing God's love offers refuge impact how you face challenges and uncertainties in life?

____

____

____

____

____

____

____

____

____

In what ways can you encourage others to find refuge in God's love during their own trials?

____

____

____

____

Week 3:

RADIATING LOVE & Compassion

Discover how God's love empowers you to show compassion to others, sharing His heart with a world in need of His kindness.

Overcoming Fear

"So do not fear, for I am with you; do not be dismayed, for I am your God. I will strengthen you and help you; I will uphold you with my righteous right hand."
Isaiah 41:10

COURAGEOUS DAUGHTER,

Imagine a father standing by his child's side, dispelling her fears with his strong presence and unwavering support; that's how your Heavenly Father assures you.

Fear is a common human experience, but your Heavenly Father invites you to cast your fears upon Him. Just as a child trusts her father's protection, trust that God is with you in every circumstance.

When fear attempts to grip your heart, remember His promise: He will strengthen, help, and uphold you. You are never alone, for your Heavenly Father's love and power surround you.

PRAYER:

Loving Father,
As I face challenges, I declare that I have not been given a spirit of fear but of power, love, and a sound mind. Help me overcome fear with the assurance of Your love and the strength found in You. In Jesus name, I pray. Amen.

What Does This Reveal About God?

This image of a father driving away his child's fears with a strong and unwavering presence reflects God as a Source of courage and assurance. **God's invitation to cast fears upon Him (Matthew 11:28), reveals His desire to be intimately involved in every aspect of His children's lives.** It reveals a God who stands beside His children, ready to provide strength and support in the face of fear and despair. His promise to strengthen, help, and uphold signifies a God who is actively involved in overcoming fear in the lives of His beloved.

How Can I Apply This to My Life?

When fear arises, consciously turn to God, casting your anxieties upon Him in prayer. 1 Peter 5:7 in the Amplified Bible (AMP), says "casting all your cares [all your anxieties, all your worries, and all your concerns, once and for all] on Him, for He cares about you [with deepest affection, and watches over you very carefully]".

Trust in God's constant presence and His unwavering support, just like a child trusting her father's protection. **Memorize and meditate on promises from Scripture that affirm God's strength and help in times of fear.** Cultivate a habit of seeking God's guidance and reassurance through prayer and the study of His Word when faced with fearful situations. Remind yourself daily that you are not alone, for your Heavenly Father's love and power surrounds you, enabling you to overcome fear with courage.

"Fear has no place in a heart that is filled with God's love. Stand strong, for He is with you."

Let's Reflect

Identify a fear that may be holding you back. How can understanding God's love help you overcome that fear?

Walking in Humility

"He has shown you, O mortal, what is good. And what does the Lord require of you? To act justly and to love mercy and to walk humbly with your God."
Micah 6:8

HUMBLE DAUGHTER,

Imagine a child walking hand in hand with her father, learning life's lessons through his guidance and experiencing his love in every step; that's the invitation to walk humbly with your Heavenly Father.

Your journey as God's daughter includes embracing humility in your interactions and attitudes. Just as a child learns humility by watching her father's example, cultivate a heart of humility that aligns with God's desires for you.

Humbly seek justice, show mercy, and follow His lead in every aspect of your life. As you walk in step with Him, you'll discover the beauty of a humble heart that reflects His character.

PRAYER:

Heavenly Father,
Teach me the way of humility. Help me to walk in the footsteps of Christ, being considerate of others and serving in a way that glorify your name. May my actions and attitudes reflect the humility found in Your sacrificial love. In Jesus name, I pray. Amen.

What Does This Reveal About God?

The image of a child walking hand in hand with her father, learning life's lessons through guidance and experiencing love in every step, **reveals God as a Father who desires a humble and teachable heart in His children.** God invites His daughters to walk in humility, mirroring the humble heart that is seen in the relationship between you and Him. This reflects God's desire for His children to embrace humility not just as a virtue but as a way of walking through life, seeking justice, showing mercy, and following His lead.

How Can I Apply This to My Life?

Study God's character in Scripture, take note of His humility and the ways He exemplifies it in interactions with His children. Another way to apply this to your life is by cultivating a teachable spirit. **Approach life's lessons recognizing that there is always room for growth and learning.**

Learn to follow God's lead as you actively pursue justice in your interactions with others, and let mercy guide your responses. **In every decision and action, seek to align yourself with God's guidance, acknowledging His wisdom as you navigate life.** As you walk in humility, your life becomes a reflection of God's character, and others will see His love through your humble and compassionate actions.

"True greatness is found in humble service. As you serve, you are a reflection of Christ."

Let's Reflect

Consider a situation in your life where humility was a virtue.
How can you embody humility in your interactions today?

Prayer and Communion

"Pray continually."
1 Thessalonians 5:17

PRAYERFUL DAUGHTER,

Imagine a child maintaining a constant conversation with her father, sharing her thoughts, hopes, and dreams; that's the essence of the prayerful relationship your Heavenly Father desires with you.

Just as a child talks openly with her father, cultivate a habit of continuous prayer. **Approach God's throne with a heart eager to converse with Him throughout your day.** Share your joys, concerns, and desires, knowing that He delights in your fellowship.

The lines of communication are always open, and as you embrace a lifestyle of prayer, you'll find that your relationship with your Heavenly Father deepens.

PRAYER:

Heavenly Father,
As I enter into prayer and communion with You, may my heart be attuned to Your voice. Speak to me, guide me, and draw me closer to Your heart. May our communion be a source of strength and intimacy. In Jesus name, I pray. Amen.

What Does This Reveal About God?

The image of a child maintaining a constant conversation with her father, sharing thoughts, hopes, and dreams, reveals God as a Father who desires an ongoing and intimate conversation with His children through prayer. **God invites His daughters to engage in a continuous dialogue with Him. An open and honest communication between a child and her father.** This reflects God's desire for a relationship marked by constant connection, where His children share their thoughts, feelings, concerns, and desires freely.

How Can I Apply This to My Life?

Develop a habit of ongoing conversation with God throughout your day, acknowledging His presence in every moment. **Approach prayer with transparency, sharing your thoughts, hopes, and dreams with God as you would with a trusted friend.** Designate specific times for focused prayer, creating sacred moments to deepen your connection with God.

Prayer is not just about speaking but also about listening. During prayer set time to just be still and listen for God to speak. Be attentive to God's voice and promptings during your moments of communion. **Recognize prayer as a form of communion with your Heavenly Father.** Allow it to be a time of closeness, where you draw near to Him and experience His presence.

"Prayer is your lifeline to the Father. In communion, you discover His heart and share your own."

Let's Reflect

How intentional are you about your prayer life? In what ways can you deepen your communion with God through prayer?

Receiving His Grace

"Let us then approach God's throne of grace with confidence, so that we may receive mercy and find grace to help us in our time of need."
Hebrews 4:16

GRACE-FILLED DAUGHTER,

Imagine a child approaching her father with confidence, knowing that his love and grace are always available; that's the invitation to approach your Heavenly Father's throne of grace.

Just as a child receives guidance and comfort from her father, approach God with confidence, especially in times of need. **His grace is abundant, and His mercy is freely given.**

There's no need to fear judgment or rejection; instead, find assurance in His loving embrace. As you receive His grace, you'll find the strength and help you need to navigate life's challenges.

PRAYER:

Gracious God,
I come before You today with a heart open to receive Your abundant grace. Remind me that Your grace is sufficient for me, and in my weakness, Your strength is made perfect. Thank You for the unmerited favor that flows from Your love. In Jesus name, I pray. Amen.

What Does This Reveal About God?

The imagery of a child approaching her father with confidence, knowing that love and grace are always available, reveals God as a Father whose throne is characterized by grace. It reflects the concept of a throne of grace, where His children can come with confidence, not fearing judgment or rejection. **This paints a picture of God's abundant grace, freely given to His daughters. It shows that His mercy is ever-available, and His love is a constant source of comfort and guidance.**

How Can I Apply This to My Life?

Approach God's throne with boldness and confidence, knowing that His grace is there for you, especially in times of need. Like a child seeking guidance and comfort from a father, turn to God in all circumstances, trusting in His love and grace. **Let go of fear and embrace the assurance of God's loving embrace.** Understand that His grace covers every aspect of your life.

In moments of difficulty, consciously receive God's grace. It provides the strength and help needed to navigate life's challenges. And remember that as you receive God's grace, extend that grace to others. **Let your interactions be characterized by the same love and compassion that you receive from your Heavenly Father.**

"Grace is the embrace of a loving Father, always ready to restore and renew."

Let's Reflect

Reflect on a moment when you experienced God's grace. How can you extend that grace to others today?

Being a Light

"You are the light of the world. A town built on a hill cannot be hidden... Let your light shine before others, that they may see your good deeds and glorify your Father in heaven."
Matthew 5:14-16

RADIANT DAUGHTER,

Imagine a child holding a lantern high, illuminating the darkness and guiding others on their path; that's the call to be a light in this world.

As a daughter of the Most High, you carry His light within you. Just as a child is a reflection of their father, you too are a reflection of your Heavenly Father.

Let your light shine before others. **Your actions, attitudes, and kindness can make a significant impact on those around you.**

By demonstrating love, compassion, and integrity, you point people toward the source of your light —your Heavenly Father. Your good deeds reflect His glory and bring honor to His name.

PRAYER:

Heavenly Father,
Thank You for being the ultimate Source of light in my life. As I seek to be a light in this world, may Your glory shine through me. Help me to reflect Your love, kindness, and joy in all that I do. Guide me to illuminate the darkness around me and lead others toward Your eternal light. In Jesus name, I pray. Amen.

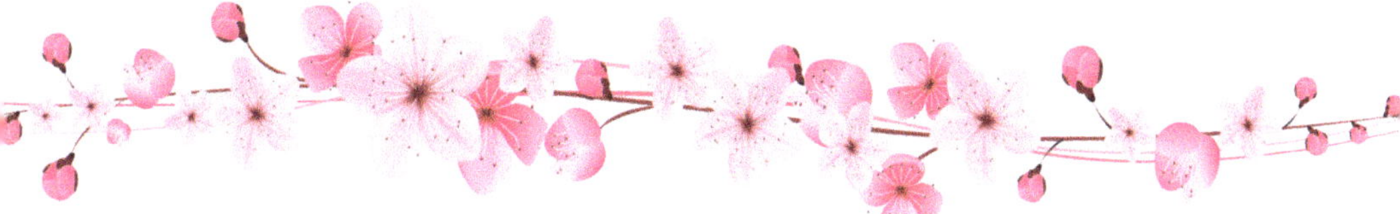

What Does This Reveal About God?

God is the ultimate source of light. In declaring that "you are the light of the world," **God emphasizes His desire for His children to radiate His love and goodness in a world often overshadowed by darkness.** The image of a town on a hill that cannot be hidden, in Matthew 5:14-16, speaks to the inherent visibility and impact of God's light within His children. As a daughter of God, your identity is deeply connected to this divine light. You are called to mirror the radiant light of your Heavenly Father in every aspect of your life.

How Can I Apply This to My Life?

Embrace your role as a bearer of God's light. Just as a lantern illuminates the darkness, let your life be a beacon of hope, kindness, and love in a world that often yearns for these qualities. **Your actions, attitudes, and choices are powerful instruments through which God's light can shine.**

In practical terms, consider how you can infuse love, compassion, and integrity into your daily interactions. Small acts of kindness and words spoken with grace can have a profound impact on those around you. **When faced with challenges, let the light of God guide your responses and decisions, allowing His love to shine through you.** Remember, your light shines brightest in the darkness. Allow God's love to spread throughout every corner of your life, becoming a testimony to His transformative power. Let your light be a reflection of His glory, drawing others closer to the source of all light—your Heavenly Father.

"Your light shines brightest in the darkness. Let God's love illuminate every corner of your life."

Let's Reflect

Where can you be a light in someone else's life today? How does being a light align with your identity as God's daughter?

Day 20

Persevering Through Trials

"Consider it pure joy, my brothers and sisters, whenever you face trials of many kinds, because you know that the testing of your faith produces perseverance. Let perseverance finish its work so that you may be mature and complete, not lacking anything."
James 1:2-4

ENDURING DAUGHTER,

Imagine a child weathering a storm with her father's steady presence, learning valuable lessons of strength and resilience; that's the journey of perseverance your Heavenly Father walks with you through.

Trials are an inevitable part of life, but God assures you that they serve a purpose. Just as a child learns to persevere through challenges, embrace trials as opportunities for growth.

Your faith is refined through adversity, producing endurance and maturity. **Trust that God walks with you through every trial, teaching you valuable lessons and molding you into a strong and complete daughter of the Most High.**

PRAYER:

Dear Lord,
In the face of trials, I turn to You, the Source of my strength. Grant me the perseverance to endure challenges, knowing that Your refining work is at play. Teach me the lessons You have in store for me through my adversity, and help me emerge stronger and more resilient. I trust in Your purpose and plan. Amen.

What Does This Reveal About God?

While trials are inevitable, God, in His wisdom, transforms them into opportunities for growth and refinement. The image of a child weathering a storm with her father's steady presence illustrates God's commitment to walking with His daughters through every challenge. **The trials you face are not random or purposeless; they are a means through which your faith is tested, refined, and strengthened.** Just as a child learns valuable lessons of strength and resilience through challenges, **God, as your Heavenly Father, guides you through trials to produce perseverance, maturity, and completeness.**

How Can I Apply This to My Life?

Instead of viewing challenges as obstacles, recognize them as opportunities for spiritual growth. Just as a child learns valuable lessons while weathering a storm with her father, **trust that God walks with you through every trial, teaching you profound lessons that contribute to your maturity.**

Allow perseverance to finish its work, trusting that, with each trial, you are being molded into a mature and complete daughter of the Most High. As a practical application, seek the lessons embedded in the challenges and maintain a posture of faith and trust, knowing that God's strength is made perfect in weakness. **Remember, trials may bend you, but they won't break you, for God's strength is indeed made perfect in your moments of weakness (Read 2 Corinthians 12:9-10).** Trust God, and let perseverance lead you toward spiritual maturity and completeness in Him.

"Trials may bend you, but they won't break you.
For His strength is made perfect in weakness."

Let's Reflect

Think about a past trial. How did God sustain you through it, and what lessons did you learn?

Reflecting His Love

"Love is patient, love is kind. It does not envy, it does not boast, it is not proud... It always protects, always trusts, always hopes, always perseveres."
1 Corinthians 13:4-7

LOVING DAUGHTER,

Imagine a child mirroring her father's love by showing patience, kindness, and unwavering care; that's the reflection of love your Heavenly Father encourages you to embody.

Love is central to your relationship with God and others. Just as a child learns from her father's example of love, strive to mirror the love described in 1 Corinthians 13. Be patient and kind, putting others' needs before your own.

Let your love be genuine, humble, and selfless, reflecting the heart of your Heavenly Father. As you extend love to those around you, you mirror His love to the world.

PRAYER:

Heavenly Father,
As I reflect on Your boundless love, may it overflow from my heart to others. Help me to embody the love described in 1 Corinthians 13—patient, kind, and selfless. Guide me in every interaction to mirror Your love, bringing glory to Your name. In Jesus' name, I pray. Amen.

What Does This Reveal About God?

This passage reveals God as the embodiment of love. It beautifully describes the attributes of divine love—patience, kindness, humility, and selflessness. The analogy of a child mirroring her father's love highlights the intimate relationship God desires with His daughters, urging them to reflect His love in their interactions with others.

God's character, as portrayed in this context, signifies that love is not merely an action but an essence flowing from His very nature. His love is patient, kind, humble, and enduring. This passage unveils God as the ultimate source and example of true, selfless love.

How Can I Apply This to My Life?

Strive to embody the qualities of love described in 1 Corinthians 13. Just as a child learns from her father's example, **let God's love be the standard by which you measure your actions and attitudes.** Be patient and kind, putting the needs of others before your own.

In your relationships, practice genuine, humble, and selfless love. Consider how you can extend love in practical ways, mirroring the heart of your Heavenly Father. As you navigate daily interactions, let God's love guide your thoughts, words, and actions. **Remember, love is the greatest mark of a true disciple.** Allow God's love to flow through you, leaving an indelible mark on the world. In every circumstance, let your love reflect the divine love that has been poured into your heart.

"Love is the greatest mark of a true disciple. Let God's love guide your thoughts, words, and actions."

Consider a challenging relationship. How can you reflect God's love in your interactions with that person?

End of Week 3
ENCOURAGEMENT:

Three weeks into 'Walking in His Love: A 30-Day Devotional for God's Daughters,' and your journey is unfolding beautifully. Like a river flowing steadily toward its destination, your heart is being guided by the currents of God's love and purpose.

This week, you've experienced transformation, forgiveness, and compassion as His daughter. As you enter this weekend, let His love fill every corner of your heart, leaving no room for doubt or fear.

Know that His plans for you are good, and His love empowers you to step into the fullness of your identity. Keep pressing on, radiant daughter, and continue to walk in His love.

Reflection Questions

Think of a recent situation where you showed kindness and compassion to someone. How did it reflect God's love?

____

____

____

____

____

____

____

____

____

____

____

____

____

What barriers sometimes prevent you from extending love and compassion to others? How can you overcome these barriers?

How can you intentionally incorporate acts of kindness and compassion into your daily life moving forward?

Week 4:

Uncover the unchanging truth of God's Word that anchors you in His love, guiding your steps and shaping your perspective.

Surrendering Control

"In their hearts humans plan their course, but the Lord establishes their steps."
Proverbs 16:9

SURRENDERED DAUGHTER,

Imagine a child offering a map to her father, trusting his guidance and allowing him to lead the way; that's the invitation to surrender control to your Heavenly Father.

Your plans and desires are important, but ultimately, God's plans surpass your own. Just as a child learns to trust her father's direction, surrender your plans to God's sovereign wisdom.

He knows the path that's best for you. And as you release your grip on control, you'll find peace in His leading and discover that His plans far exceed your expectations.

PRAYER:

Dear Lord,
I surrender my plans and desires to Your sovereign wisdom. Grant me the humility to trust Your leading in every aspect of my life. May Your plans, which surpass my own, guide me toward a path filled with purpose and peace. I release control to You, knowing that Your ways are higher. Amen.

What Does This Reveal About God?

Today's devotional reveals God as the sovereign orchestrator of our lives. The analogy of a child handing over a map to her father and trusting his guidance beautifully captures the essence of surrendering control to our Heavenly Father. **It emphasizes the divine truth that, while we may plan our course, it is the Lord who establishes our steps (Proverbs 16:9).** God's character, as revealed in this context, signifies His omniscient (all-knowing) wisdom and His divine guidance. **God invites His daughters to trust Him with their plans, understanding that His ways surpass human understanding (Isaiah 55:8).**

How Can I Apply This to My Life?

Reflect on your plans and desires, and then surrender them to God. Much like a child offering a map to her father, trust in God's guidance and let Him lead the way. Acknowledge that, while your plans are significant, God's plans far exceed your own. **As you release your grip on control, find peace in God's leading. Embrace the truth that His ways are higher, and His love is your guiding force.**

Allow surrender to be an ongoing practice in your life, recognizing that God's plans are filled with wisdom, purpose, and love. **Remember, surrendering control is not a sign of weakness but an expression of trust in the One who knows the path that's best for you.** Surrender your plans to the Author of your story and let His divine guidance shape your journey.

"Surrender your plans to the Author of your story. His ways are higher, and His love is your guide."

Let's Reflect

In what areas of your life do you struggle to surrender control? How might surrendering align with your identity as God's daughter?

Bearing Each Other's Burdens

"Carry each other's burdens, and in this way you will fulfill the law of Christ."
Galatians 6:2

SUPPORTIVE DAUGHTER,

Imagine a child lending a helping hand to her father, sharing in his responsibilities and offering support; that's the essence of bearing each other's burdens.

Your Heavenly Father calls you to walk alongside others, just as He walks alongside you. Just as a child participates in her father's work, share the burdens of those around you.

Offer a listening ear, extend a helping hand, and pray for one another. In doing so, you fulfill Christ's command to love one another. **Your acts of compassion reflect the heart of your Heavenly Father.**

PRAYER:

Loving Father,

As I bear the burdens of others, may Your compassion flow through me. Teach me to walk alongside my brothers and sisters, showing empathy in their struggles and offering support. Let my actions reflect Your love, and may I fulfill Christ's command to carry one another's burdens. In Jesus name. Amen.

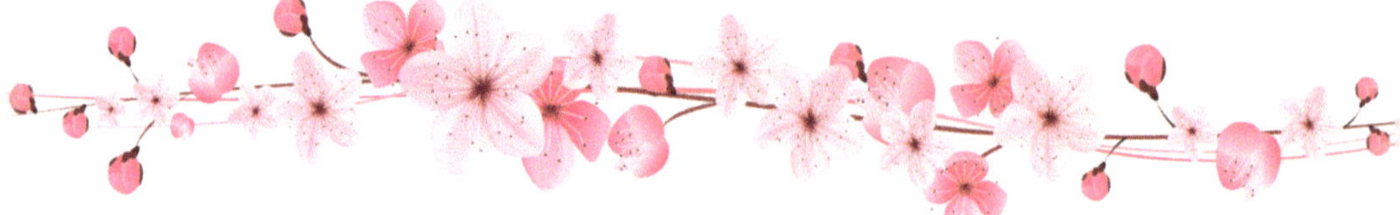

What Does This Reveal About God?

The analogy of a child lending a helping hand to her father, sharing in his responsibilities and offering support, reveals God as a Father who invites His children to actively engage in His work. To be about their Father's business (Luke 2:49). **It depicts God as a relational and compassionate Father who desires His children to walk alongside one another, just as He walks alongside each one of them.** This imagery emphasizes the call to share in the burdens of others, reflecting the communal and supportive nature of God's family.

How Can I Apply This to My Life?

Actively engage in the lives of those around you. **Offer your presence and support in both good times and challenging moments.** Be willing to share the burdens of others. This could be through practical assistance, a listening ear, or heartfelt prayers. Reflect the compassion of your Heavenly Father in your interactions.

Approach others with kindness and empathy. **Recognize that by sharing burdens, you fulfill Christ's command to love one another.** Your actions become a tangible expression of Christ's love in the world. Lift up the concerns and needs of others in prayer. Intercede on the behalf of others, knowing that prayer is a powerful way to support one another.

"By lifting another's burden, you embody Christ's love. Your kindness brings healing and hope."

Let's Reflect

Reflect on a time when someone helped bear your burden. How can you do the same for others?

Day 24

Walking in Wisdom

"If any of you lacks wisdom, you should ask God, who gives generously to all without finding fault, and it will be given to you."
James 1:5

WISE DAUGHTER,

Imagine a child seeking her father's advice when faced with a difficult decision, trusting his wisdom and guidance; that's the invitation to seek wisdom from your Heavenly Father.

Just as a child values her father's counsel, recognize your need for God's wisdom in every aspect of life. When you lack understanding, ask Him for insight. **God invites you to approach Him with your questions and uncertainties.**

As you seek His wisdom, remember that He gives generously without judgment. His desire is to guide you toward decisions that align with His perfect will. **Trust that His wisdom, which surpasses human understanding, will illuminate your path and help you navigate life's complexities.**

PRAYER:

God of Wisdom,
I seek Your guidance in every decision. Grant me discernment and understanding as I navigate life's complexities. In moments of uncertainty, I turn to You for wisdom that surpasses human understanding. Thank You for being the source of true and perfect wisdom. Amen.

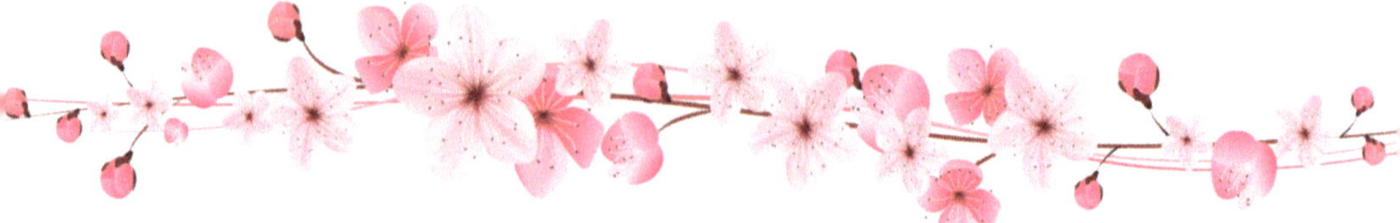

What Does This Reveal About God?

The image of a child seeking her father's advice and trusting in his wisdom unveils God as a Father who invites His children to seek His guidance. This reveals God's availability and willingness to offer wisdom to those who approach Him. **The analogy presents God as the ultimate Source of wisdom, emphasizing His desire to guide His children through life's complexities.** The generosity with which He provides wisdom reflects His boundless love and care.

How Can I Apply This to My Life?

Acknowledge that, like a child seeking a father's counsel, you need God's wisdom in your life. Just as a child approaches her father with questions, **go to God with your uncertainties, decisions, and concerns. Actively seek your Father's divine insight.** Pray for wisdom in specific situations, trusting that God will provide clarity.

Remember that God gives wisdom generously and without judgment. Trust in His willingness to guide you. **Strive to make decisions that align with God's perfect will.** Seek His guidance in every aspect of your life. Wisdom often unfolds over time. Be patient, allowing God's guidance to manifest in His perfect timing.

"Choose God's wisdom over worldly advice. In His guidance, you find the path to abundant life."

How do you seek and apply God's wisdom in your decision-making? In what areas of your life do you need His guidance today?

Clothed in Strength

"It is God who arms me with strength and keeps my way secure."
Psalm 18:32

STRONG DAUGHTER,

Imagine a child being handed a shield by her father, equipped to face challenges with confidence and assurance; that's the strength your Heavenly Father provides.

Just as a father empowers his child with protection, **God arms you with His strength. He is your source of unwavering power, and He keeps your way secure.**

Just as a child trusts her father's ability to shield her, rely on God's strength in times of adversity. **His presence empowers you to overcome obstacles and walk with courage, knowing that He is your ever-present help.**

PRAYER:

Mighty God,
Clothe me in Your strength as I face the challenges of this day. You are my shield and fortress, and in Your strength, I find courage. Help me to rely on Your power, knowing that, with You by my side, I am more than a conqueror. In Jesus powerful name, I pray. Amen.

What Does This Reveal About God?

The image of a child being handed a shield by her father illustrates God as a provider of strength and protection. This reveals God's role as a Source of unwavering power, emphasizing His commitment to equipping His children for life's challenges. **The analogy paints a picture of God as a protector**, securing the path of those who trust in His strength. It showcases **God's reliability as an ever-present help**, ready to empower His children to face adversity with courage.

How Can I Apply This to My Life?

Acknowledge that your strength comes from God. Like a child relying on her father, recognize your dependence on God's power. Actively seek God's strength in times of adversity. **Turn to Him in prayer, asking for the courage and assurance that come from His unwavering power.** Just as a child trusts her father's ability to shield her, trust in God's protection. Believe that His strength will carry you through challenges.

Allow God's strength to empower you to face challenges with courage. Step forward knowing that you are equipped by the Almighty. **Rely on God's ever-present help**. In moments of difficulty, turn to His presence for guidance, assurance, and strength. Just as a father empowers his child, encourage others with the strength you've received from God. **Be a source of support and inspiration for those around you.**

"In God's strength, you are an overcomer. When you're weak, He's strong on your behalf."

Let's Reflect

Identify a recent situation where you felt weak. How can you rely on God's strength in similar circumstances?

Reflecting His Holiness

"But just as He who called you is holy, so be holy in all you do; for it is written: 'Be holy, because I am holy.'"
1 Peter 1:15-16

HOLY DAUGHTER,

Imagine a child imitating her father's actions and words, aspiring to reflect his character in every way; that's the call to reflect God's holiness in your life. Just as a child mirrors her father's behavior, strive to embody the holiness described in Scripture.

Your Heavenly Father is holy, and He invites you to align your thoughts, words, and actions with His holy nature. Pursue a life of integrity, righteousness, and purity, letting His holiness shine through you.

As you walk in holiness, you become a living testimony of God's transformative power.

PRAYER:

Holy Father,
As I strive to be holy as You are holy, purify my thoughts, words, and actions. Let Your holiness shine through me, transforming me into a reflection of Your character. Thank You for the sanctifying work You are doing in my life. In Jesus name, I pray. Amen.

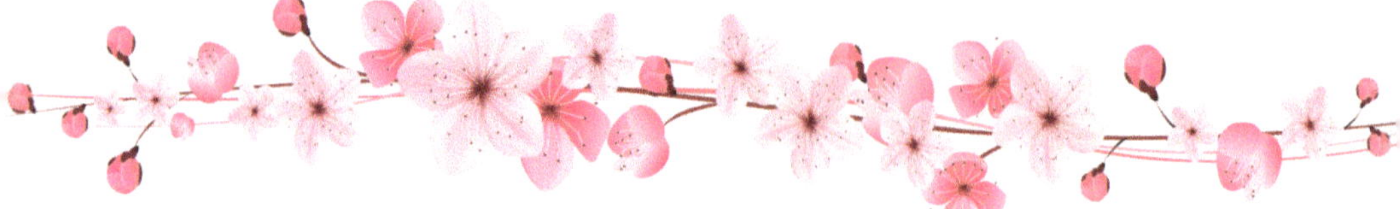

What Does This Reveal About God?

The analogy of a child imitating her father's actions to reflect his character illustrates God's call for His children to mirror His holiness. **It reveals God as the embodiment of holiness, setting a standard for purity, righteousness, and integrity.** God's holiness is not just a distant attribute but an invitation for believers to align their lives with His divine nature. **The image reveals God as a Source of transformation, emphasizing that walking in holiness is a testament to His sanctifying work in the lives of His children.**

How Can I Apply This to My Life?

Acknowledge God's holiness as the standard for your life. Understand that He calls you to a life of purity, righteousness, and integrity. **Strive to align every aspect of your life—your thoughts, words, and actions—with God's holiness. Let His character permeate every area of your existence.** Understand the attributes of God's holiness by immersing yourself in Scripture. Let the Word of God guide and shape your understanding of a holy life. Seek your Father's transformative power in your life. Pray for the Holy Spirit to mold you into a person who reflects the holiness of your Heavenly Father. Make intentional choices that reflect God's holiness. **Practice integrity in your dealings and pursue righteousness in your actions.** As you walk in holiness, become a living testimony of God's transformative power. **Let your life witness to the sanctifying work of God in you.** Inspire and encourage others to pursue holiness. Share your journey and experiences to uplift and support fellow believers in their pursuit of a holy life.

"Holiness is a reflection of God's character in you. As you grow in the likeness of Christ, His love shines through."

How does the concept of reflecting God's holiness resonate
with you? In what ways can you embody holiness in your
actions?

Day 27

Restoring Relationships

"Bear with each other and forgive one another if any of you has a grievance against someone. Forgive as the Lord forgave you. And over all these virtues put on love, which binds them all together in perfect unity."
Colossians 3:13-14

RESTORED DAUGHTER,

Imagine a child extending a hand of reconciliation to her sibling after a disagreement, choosing forgiveness over bitterness; that's the call to restore relationships as your Heavenly Father restores you.

Forgiveness is a cornerstone of your relationship with God and others. Just as a child learns from her father's example of forgiveness, choose to forgive as the Lord forgave you.

Extend grace to those who have hurt you, knowing that you, too, have been forgiven. **Through forgiveness, you mirror the heart of your Heavenly Father, and love becomes the binding force that unites hearts in unity.**

PRAYER:

Gracious Lord,
Grant me the strength and humility to forgive as You have forgiven me. Guide me in the work of restoration, whether in my relationship with You or with others. Let love be the binding force that unites hearts in perfect unity. In the name of Jesus, I pray. Amen.

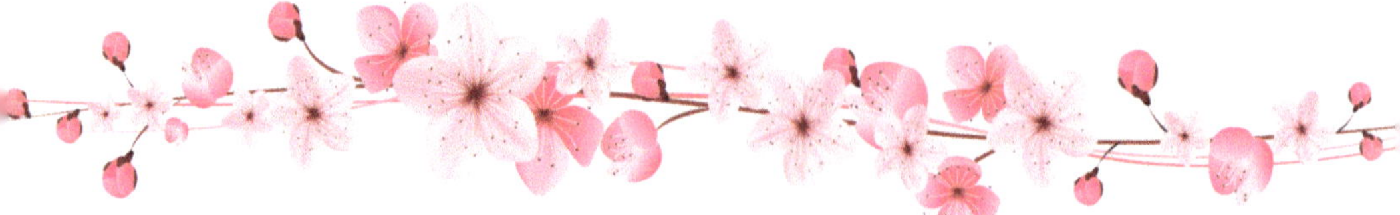

What Does This Reveal About God?

The image of a child extending a hand of reconciliation after a disagreement mirrors God's heart for restoring relationships. **It reveals God as the ultimate Source of forgiveness and restoration, drawing a parallel between a child's act of forgiveness and how God forgives His children.** God's nature is revealed as One of grace, mercy, and a willingness to restore broken connections. The analogy emphasizes forgiveness as a cornerstone of the relationship with God and others, highlighting the transformative power of God's forgiveness in the believer's life.

How Can I Apply This to My Life?

Take time to reflect on the forgiveness you've received from God. Understand the depth of His mercy and grace in your own life. When faced with conflicts or disagreements, choose forgiveness over bitterness. **Echo God's forgiveness by extending grace to others, just as He has graciously forgiven you.** Be proactive in restoring broken relationships. Extend a hand of reconciliation, just as the child in the example reaches out to her sibling. Recognize the power of love in restoring and maintaining relationships. Let love be the binding force that unites hearts in unity, mirroring the unconditional love God has shown you. **Pray for a heart that forgives readily. Ask God for the strength and humility to forgive others as He has forgiven you.** Practice extending grace to those who may have hurt you. Actively work towards unity in your relationships. Be a motivator for reconciliation and healing, reflecting the restoration you've experienced through your Heavenly Father.

"Restoration is a work of grace. As you reconcile, you echo God's heart for unity and healing."

Consider a strained relationship in your life. How might God's love guide you in taking steps toward restoration?

____

____

____

____

____

____

____

____

____

____

____

____

____

____

____

____

____

Abundant Life

"The thief comes only to steal and kill and destroy; I have come that they may have life, and have it to the full."
John 10:10

ABUNDANT DAUGHTER,

Imagine a child exploring the wonders of creation with her father, embracing every moment with excitement and awe; that's the invitation to experience an abundant life in your Heavenly Father's presence.

Your Heavenly Father desires for you to live life to the fullest. Just as a father wants his child to experience joy, God intends for you to experience His abundant love, joy, and purpose.

Reject the lies of the enemy that seek to steal your joy and replace them with the truth of God's promises. Embrace the abundant life that comes from walking closely with your Heavenly Father.

PRAYER:

Heavenly Father,
Thank You for the invitation to live life to the fullest in Your presence. I reject the lies that seek to steal my joy and embrace the abundant life You offer. Fill my days with Your love, joy, and purpose. In Jesus' name, I pray. Amen.

What Does This Reveal About God?

The imagery of a child exploring the wonders of creation with her father reflects God's desire for His children to experience an abundant life. **It reveals God as a loving Father who takes delight in seeing His children embrace life with excitement and awe.** The invitation to abundant life in the presence of your Heavenly Father reveals God's intention for His children to live life to the fullest. His character is depicted as one that desires joy, love, and purpose for each believer, emphasizing the abundance that comes from a close relationship with Him.

How Can I Apply This to My Life?

Acknowledge and embrace the abundant love that God has for you. Understand that His love is a Source of joy and fulfillment. Engage in activities that bring you closer to Him and allow you to experience His presence in a joyful way. Recognize that God has a purpose for your life. Seek His guidance in discovering and fulfilling that purpose. Live with intentionality and alignment with His plans. Be aware of lies and negative influences that seek to steal your joy. **Reject thoughts or beliefs that are contrary to God's promises. Guard your mind against negativity. Immerse yourself in the truth of God's promises. Meditate on Scripture and let His Word shape your perspective.** The closer you walk with your Father, the more you'll experience the abundance He offers. As you experience God's abundance, share it with others. Be a source of joy, love, and encouragement to those around you.

"Abundant life is found in Him alone. Embrace His promises and live with purpose and passion."

What does an abundant life mean to you? How can you embrace that abundance in God today?

Sharing God's Love

"We love because he first loved us."
1 John 4:19

LOVING DAUGHTER,

Imagine a child offering her toys to a friend, reflecting her father's generosity and kindness; that's the invitation to share God's love with others.

Your capacity to love others is rooted in the love you've received from your Heavenly Father.

Just as a child can learn to share from her father's example, extend love to those around you. **As you experience God's boundless love, let it flow through you in your actions, words, and interactions.** By sharing His love, you become a channel of His grace and compassion to a world that's desperately in need.

PRAYER:

Loving Father,
As I share Your boundless love, open my heart to be a vessel of Your grace and compassion. Guide my words and actions to reflect Your love to those around me. May my life be a testimony to the transformative power of Your love. Amen.

What Does This Reveal About God?

The example of a child offering her toys to a friend, mirroring the generosity and kindness she learned from her father, unveils God's nature as the ultimate Source of love and compassion. **This illustrates God as a Father who models selfless love and invites His children to emulate that love in their relationships.** The act of sharing reflects the overflow of God's boundless love onto others, emphasizing the notion that our capacity to love is deeply rooted in the love we've received from our Heavenly Father. **God's character is one of generosity, and He encourages His children to share His love generously with those around them.**

How Can I Apply This to My Life?

Acknowledge and embrace the love you've received from God. Understand that His love is the foundation for your ability to love others. Imitate God's generosity and kindness in your actions. Extend acts of kindness to those around you. **Small gestures of love, empathy, and consideration can have a significant impact on others.** Pay attention to the needs of those around you. Actively listen and be sensitive to opportunities where you can share God's love by meeting practical or emotional needs. **Engage in acts of service without expecting anything in return. When you serve selflessly, you mirror God's sacrificial love.** Lift others up in prayer. Intercede on their behalf, seeking God's blessings for them. Share the message of God's love through your life and words. Be intentional about introducing others to the Source of your love and joy—your relationship with God.

"Share God's love without hesitation. Your words and actions have the power to change lives."

Reflect on opportunities to share God's love. How can you intentionally be a conduit of His love to others?

Trusting God's Plan

"For I know the plans I have for you, declares the Lord, plans to prosper you and not to harm you, plans to give you hope and a future."
Jeremiah 29:11

SUBMITTED DAUGHTER,

Imagine a child excitedly unpacking a gift from her father, trusting that it holds something wonderful and purposeful; that's the assurance of God's plan for your life.

Your Heavenly Father knows you intimately and has a plan uniquely designed just for you.

Just as a child trusts her father's loving intentions, trust that God's plans are for your good. **Even when circumstances seem uncertain, remember His promise of hope and a future.** As you surrender your desires to His sovereign will, you'll experience the fulfillment of His purpose and the abundant life He has prepared for you.

PRAYER:

Faithful Father,
As I trust in Your plan, help me surrender my desires to Your sovereign will. I place my uncertainties in Your hands, trusting that Your plans are for my good. Thank You for the hope and future You promise. In Jesus name, I pray. Amen.

What Does This Reveal About God?

The analogy of a child opening a gift from her father sheds light on God's detailed and purposeful plan for each individual. **It reveals God as a loving Father who intimately knows His children and carefully designs a plan that is both wonderful and meaningful.** The comparison emphasizes the trust a child places in her father, mirroring the trust God desires from His children regarding His plans. **God's plans are not arbitrary; they are tailored to bring about goodness, hope, and a fulfilling future (Jeremiah 29:11).** This reveals God as an intentional and loving architect of our lives, weaving a narrative that surpasses our understanding.

How Can I Apply This to My Life?

Embrace the understanding that God is sovereign and has a unique plan for your life. **Surrender your desires and plans to God. Let go of the need to control every aspect of your life, trusting that God's plan is far better than your own.** When faced with uncertainty, anchor your hope in God's promise of a future filled with hope and goodness. Let Scripture be a source of encouragement and assurance. **God's timing may differ from your own. Practice patience as you wait for His plans to unfold, knowing that His timing is perfect.** Recall moments when God has been faithful in the past. Remind yourself of His trustworthiness as you face the future. Understand that God's plan is complexly connected to His purpose for your life. Seek to align your goals and aspirations with His greater purpose. Each step you take is a part of God's unfolding purpose.

"Trust your Father, Who is the Author of your story, for His plan is filled with hope and a future beyond your imagination."

Let's Reflect

Consider your dreams and plans. In what ways can you entrust them to God, trusting in His perfect plan for your life?

End of Week 4

ENCOURAGEMENT:

You've journeyed through four weeks of 'Walking in His Love: A 30-Day Devotional for God's Daughters,' and your transformation is becoming a radiant reflection of God's heart.

Just as a diamond is refined under pressure, you've been shaped by His love into a vessel of His grace and compassion. As you rest this weekend, remember that your Heavenly Father's love never wavers. His promises remain steadfast, and His plans for you are filled with hope.

I pray these devotionals will continue to guide and inspire you in your journey of building and strengthening your Father-daughter relationship with God.

Embrace your identity as a cherished daughter of the Most High, and allow His love, wisdom, and guidance to shape every aspect of your life.

139

Reflect on a time when a specific truth from God's Word brought you comfort or guidance. How does His truth anchor you in His love?

Are there areas in your life where you're not aligning with God's truth? How can you bring those areas into alignment with His Word?

How can you prioritize daily engagement with God's Word to deepen your understanding of His love and truth?

Reflecting on Your Journey

As you reach the end of "Walking in His Love: A 30-Day Devotional for God's Daughters," take a moment to reflect on the profound journey you've traveled. Through the highs and lows, the moments of revelation and introspection, you've immersed yourself in the embrace of your Heavenly Father's love. Your heart has been stirred, your spirit renewed, and your identity reshaped.

Consider the moments when His love felt tangible, when His words spoke directly to your soul, and when you felt the comforting refuge of His presence. Each day was a step closer to understanding the depth of your identity as a cherished daughter of God, intricately woven into the fabric of His divine plan.

Moving Forward with Renewed Faith

As you move forward from this transformative experience, the seeds of spiritual and emotional growth have been planted, and now is the time to nurture them with intentionality. Renew your commitment to embracing your God-given identity and purpose with boldness. Let the lessons learned during these 30 days guide your steps as you navigate the path ahead. Trust in the unchanging truths of God's Word, find strength in His love, and radiate His compassion in all that you do.

May this conclusion not mark the end but a new beginning—a launching pad for a life lived fully as a daughter of the Most High God. As you carry the insights gained from this devotional into your future, may your journey be marked by a deeper connection with your Heavenly Father, an unwavering faith, and a profound sense of purpose. May your steps be guided by His love, and may you continue to walk boldly in the assurance of your identity as His cherished daughter.

ACKNOWLEDGMENTS

First and foremost, I express my deepest gratitude to my Heavenly Father, the source of all wisdom and love. Your guidance has been illuminating every word and shaping the essence of this devotional. It is by Your grace that these pages breathe life into the hearts of those seeking a deeper connection with You.

To my family and friends, thank you for your unwavering support and understanding during the moments when I retreated into the sacred space of creation. Your encouragement fueled my commitment to share the transformative messages within these pages.

To the readers who embark on this journey, may you find comfort, inspiration, and divine revelation within these pages. Your willingness to explore the depths of faith is an honor and a testament to the shared pursuit of spiritual growth.

May the impact of this devotional ripple far beyond the pages and touch the lives of many.

Thank you all! May the love and grace of our Heavenly Father embrace you always.

With heartfelt gratitude,
Lapasha

DEAR DAUGHTER OF GOD,

Congratulations! You've reached the end of an incredible journey through "Walking in His Love: A 30-Day Devotional for God's Daughters." Your dedication and commitment to this transformative experience is truly inspiring.

As you reflect upon these past 30 days, may you carry with you the deep truths of God's love, the strength of your identity as His cherished daughter, and the wisdom you've gained from His Word. It is my hope that this devotional has brought you closer to your Heavenly Father and empowered you to walk confidently in your God-given identity and purpose.

Remember, this is just the beginning of your lifelong journey of growth and connection with your Father. His love will continue to guide and shape you in beautiful ways.

Thank you for investing your time, heart, and spirit into this devotional. We celebrate your journey, your growth, and your unwavering commitment to becoming the woman God created you to be.

With love and blessings, *XOXO,*

Lapasha